LIVING THINGS

ROBERT SNEDDEN

Flower

W
FRANKLIN WATTS
LONDON•SYDNEY

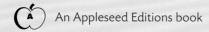 An Appleseed Editions book

First published in 2007 by Franklin Watts
338 Euston Road, London NW1 3BH

Franklin Watts Australia
Hachette Children's Books
Level 17/207 Kent St, Sydney, NSW 2000

© 2007 Appleseed Editions

Created by Appleseed Editions Ltd,
Well House, Friars Hill, Guestling,
East Sussex TN35 4ET

Designed by Guy Callaby
Edited by Pip Morgan
Illustrations by Guy Callaby
Picture research by Su Alexander

ISBN 978 07496 7553 0

Dewey Classification: 582.13

A CIP catalogue for this book is available from the British Library.

Picture acknowledgements

Title page Aflo/Nature Picture Library; 3 George D. Lepp/Corbis; 4 Richard Cummins/Corbis; 5 Paul
A.Souders/Corbis; 6 Bernard Castelein/Nature Picture Library; 7t Jean E. Roche/Nature Picture Library,
b Phil Schermeister/Corbis; 9t Guy Callaby, b Roger Tidman/Corbis; 10 Visuals Unlimited/Corbis;
11t Geoff Simpson/Nature Picture Library, b Galen Rowell/Corbis; 13 John Dransfield; 14 George D.
Lepp/Corbis; 15t Lester Lefkowitz/Corbis, b Neil Lucas/Nature Picture Library; 16 Bob Krist/Corbis;
17t Lester V.Bergman/Corbis, b Kennan Ward/Corbis; 18 Anup Shah/Nature Picture Library; 19t Tony
Wharton/Frank Lane Picture Agency/Corbis, b Science Source/Science Photo Library; 21t Duncan
McEwan/Nature Picture Library, b Aflo/Nature Picture Library; 22 Guenter Rossenbach/Zefa/Corbis;
23 Geoff Simpson/Nature Picture Library; 24t DK Limited/Corbis, b Kenneth R. Robertson; 25t Tom
Mangelsen/Nature Picture Library, b Guy Callaby; 27 Photowood Inc/Corbis; 28 Jeff Foott/Nature
Picture Library; 29 Kazuyoshi Nomachi/Corbis.

Front Cover: William Manning/Corbis

Printed in China

Franklin Watts is a division of Hachette Children's Books,
an Hachette Livre UK company

Contents

What is a flower?

When you think of flowers what comes to mind? Do you think of the brightly-coloured and pleasant-smelling plants that cheer up our parks and gardens in the spring and summer? Do you think of flowers in bunches to give as a gift?

The variety of flowering plants

There are around 250,000 different kinds of flowering plant in the world. The enormous variety includes potatoes, oak trees, parsley – even grass. Flowering plants range in size from tiny duckweeds that float on streams and ponds to eucalyptus trees that grow to heights of 90 metres.

Flowers aren't just nice to have around. Without them we would starve. All our fruits and vegetables, rice and beans, and all the grains we eat, such as oats, barley and wheat, come from flowering plants.

BELOW *A carpet of bluebonnets are an unmistakable sign that spring has arrived in Texas.*

Parts of a plant

Often when people think of a bunch of flowers they don't give much thought to the rest of the plant. But a flower is just one part of a flowering plant. As well as its flowers, a flowering plant also has leaves and roots and a stem, and each part is as important as the others. In this book we will look at all the parts of a flowering plant, not just its flowers.

The enormous variety of flowering plants, from rare and exotic orchids to the widespread dandelion, have certain things in common, because they all perform the same tasks. Here we'll discover just what a plant has to do to live and grow.

RIGHT *Australia's eucalyptus trees are the world's tallest flowering plants.*

Plants without flowers

In this book we are looking at a particular kind of plant – flowering plants – but not all plants have flowers. Here we take a brief look at plants that don't have flowers.

Mosses

These are small plants that grow close to the ground in damp and shady places. They often grow together in large numbers that form mats or clumps on a forest floor. They do not have roots but are anchored to the ground by thin tubes. They don't have stems either. Mosses reproduce by producing tiny spores that grow into new plants. There are around 19,000 different types of moss and similar plants such as liverworts and hornworts.

ABOVE *Mosses, like this hair moss, don't have flowers. They produce spores from long stalks.*

6

Ferns

Ferns have roots and stems and a number of long, thin leaves, called fronds, growing from either side of the stem. They do not produce flowers, but form spores on the undersides of their fronds. Ferns need moist conditions to survive and almost all the world's ferns – there are about 12,000 types – grow in tropical forests. Some can grow as much as 25 metres tall.

RIGHT *Tree ferns stand tall in the rainforest on the island of La Reunion in the Indian Ocean.*

Hikers walk along a trail through a forest of giant sequoias. The immense size of the trees make the hikers seem small.

Naked seeds

Plants called gymnosperms produce seeds but don't have flowers. The name gymnosperm means 'naked seed' – their seeds are not protected by fruits, as those of flowering plants are. Most gymnosperms are shrubs or trees.

The most common gymnosperms are conifers, or evergreen trees, such as pine, spruce and cedar. Most conifers have needle-like leaves, which are an adaptation to the cold conditions of the northern forests where many live. The gymnosperms also include giant redwood trees and sequoias, which are the biggest plants on the planet. There are about 750 different types of gymnosperm.

WOW!

The most massive living thing in the world is a giant sequoia tree called General Sherman, which grows in California. It is more than 83 metres tall and may weigh about 2,000 tonnes. The biggest animal, the blue whale, weighs around 125 tonnes.

Underground anchors

Some of the most important parts of a flowering plant are usually hidden from sight, and yet they may be the biggest part of the plant, holding it firmly in place. These are the plant's roots.

Essential roots

Keeping a plant anchored to the ground is important, but roots also do another essential job. When a seed sprouts the root is the first thing to appear. The plant sends out its roots through the ground, searching for the water and minerals it needs to grow.

FIBROUS ROOT SYSTEM

A fibrous root system has a number of roots of similar size that branch out through the soil.

TAPROOT SYSTEM

A taproot system has one main root that pushes down into the soil. Smaller roots branch out from it.

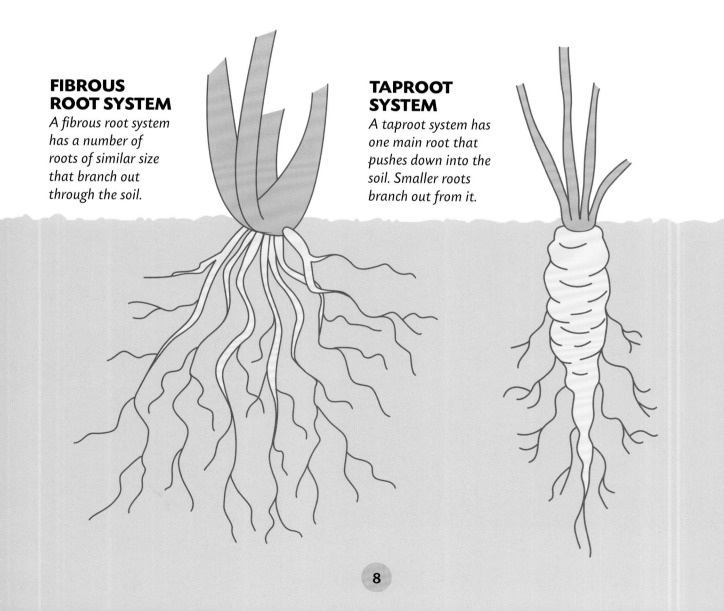

Carrots have a taproot system. Food stored in the roots provide us with a tasty vegetable.

Main roots and branching roots

Some types of plant have one main root that goes deep into the soil. This is called a taproot. Smaller branch roots grow out from the taproot. The taproot is often used as a food store by the plant. Some vegetables we eat, such as beetroots, are actually taproots.

Other plants have a great many small roots that spread out through the soil. These are called fibrous roots. Grasses have fibrous root systems. Plants with fibrous roots are difficult to pull up.

Root hairs

Roots grow from their tips. The growing tip of a root is protected by a dome-shaped root cap that pushes forwards into the soil. Just behind the tip there are root hairs that extend out and cling tightly to the soil particles. A plant might have billions of root hairs, which greatly increase the surface area through which it absorbs water and minerals. As the root pushes through the soil the root hairs are continually rubbed off and replaced. Some plants grow 100 million new root hairs every day.

Inside the roots there are tubes that carry water and minerals up from the roots to the rest of the plant. Other tubes bring food down from the leaves for storage and to provide the roots with the energy they need to grow. The water-carrying tubes are called xylem and the food-carrying tubes are called phloem.

RIGHT *Erosion of the soil has exposed the spreading roots of these pine trees. Ninety per cent of a pine tree's roots are in the top half metre of soil.*

WOW!

The deepest roots are those of plants growing in dry regions – they may have to go down a long way to find water. The roots of a wild fig tree growing in South Africa went down 120 metres into the ground.

Support above ground

Almost all flowering plants have stems that usually grow upright and provide support above the ground for the plant's buds, leaves, flowers and fruits.

Main pipeline

Stems can vary in size and appearance from the stubby stem of a cabbage to the tall trunk of a tree. The stem is the main pipeline in the plant's transport system, carrying water, minerals and food in the form of sugars to the various parts of the plant. It is like the plant's main artery.

Creeping stems

The stems of some plants, such as strawberries, creep along the ground. These stems are called runners. The stems of some other plants, such as irises, grow under the ground. These are called rhizomes and they send up new shoots and leaves to grow above ground.

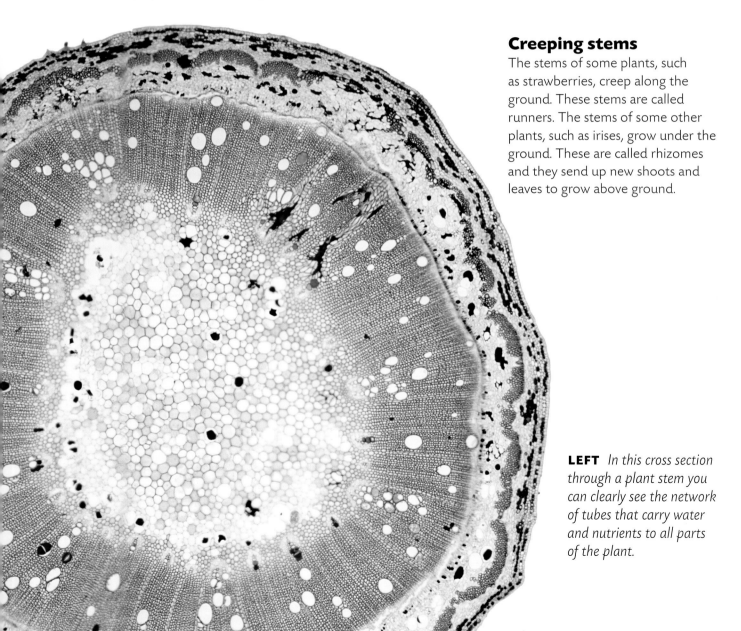

LEFT *In this cross section through a plant stem you can clearly see the network of tubes that carry water and nutrients to all parts of the plant.*

Growing buds

A plant stem produces buds from which new shoots, leaves and flowers grow. Buds first appear at the tip of the growing stem and later also appear where older leaves are attached to the stem. As it grows the bud may be protected by bud scales, which are a special type of leaf. As the new leaves develop, the stem holds them in the best position to catch the most sunlight.

LEFT *A new leaf opens out from its bud on this European beech tree.*

RIGHT *Bamboo plants grow from underground rhizomes that send up new shoots.*

Waterproofing

All stems have a waterproof coat so that the water moving up from the roots isn't lost. Most plants have a thin waxy covering, while woody plants, such as trees and shrubs, have a bark coating to protect the stem. Some plants grow spines or thorns on their stems to discourage animals from eating them.

Stem stores

Cacti and other plants that grow in dry places use their stems as water stores. Other plants use their stems to store food. Bulbs, such as onions, are actually short stems surrounded by fleshy leaves. Tubers, such as potatoes, are another form of underground stem storage. The 'eyes' on a potato are actually the beginnings of buds that will form new leaves.

Leaves

All of a plant's leaves together make up its foliage. Leaves come in many different shapes and sizes, depending on the type of plant and the conditions it grows in.

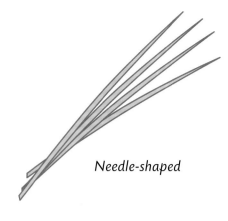

Needle-shaped

The parts of a leaf

The leaves of most flowering plants have two main parts. Most leaves have a short stalk that holds the leaf out from the stem. This is the leafstalk, or petiole. Not all flowering plants have petioles. Grasses, for example, have none. Some flowering plants have very large petioles. If you munch a stick of celery you're actually eating a petiole.

The flat part of the leaf is called the blade. Often you can see a network of veins running through the blade. These are parts of the plant's transport system, carrying food and water back and forth between the leaves and the roots. These veins are tough and strong and also help to prevent the leaf from collapsing or tearing.

Triangle-shaped

LEAF SHAPES

A typical plant leaf is broad and oval-shaped. There are many variations in the size and shape of leaves, as you can see from the selection on these pages.

Leaf shapes

Leaves come in a huge variety of shapes. They may be simple leaves, with just one blade on the leafstalk, or compound leaves, with two or more blades. A leaf can be narrow and sword-shaped, like a blade of grass, or big and round, like the floating leaf of a water lily. Many leaves are roughly oval in shape, but there are also many with complex shapes.

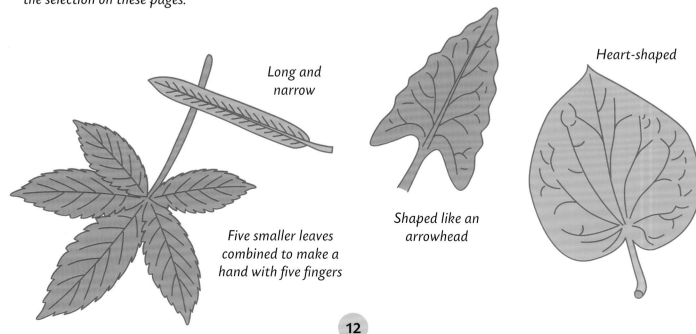

Long and narrow

Heart-shaped

Five smaller leaves combined to make a hand with five fingers

Shaped like an arrowhead

WOW!

The world's biggest leaves grow on palm trees. The massive leaves of the African raffia palm are 24 metres long. At the other end of the scale, pygmy weed, found in California, has pinhead-sized leaves that are just over a millimetre across.

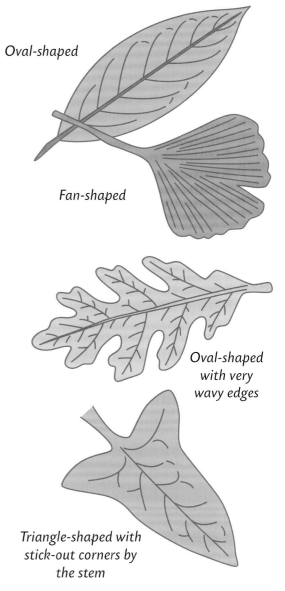

Oval-shaped

Fan-shaped

Oval-shaped with very wavy edges

Triangle-shaped with stick-out corners by the stem

Leaf surface

Like the stem, the plant's leaves are covered in a waxy waterproof coating called a cuticle. However, the leaves can't be entirely sealed because, like other living things, plants need air. There are many tiny openings, or pores, in a leaf's surface. The plant can open these to let in air and close them to save water.

Food for free

A plant's leaves are its food factories. Making food is the most important job the leaves do. They gather energy from sunlight and use it to make sugar. This process is called photosynthesis.

First link in the chain

All living things share certain things in common and one of these is that they all need energy. Animals get their energy from the food they eat, but plants are special because they can make their own food. They capture the energy of sunlight and store it in their leaves, stalks, fruits and roots.

This energy is then available first to animals that eat the plants and then to animals that eat the plant-eaters. This is a food chain. In almost all cases the first link in a food chain is a plant.

BELOW *This lush rainforest on the Caribbean island of Grenada is only a tiny fraction of the staggering amount of plant growth on the Earth.*

Making glucose

Plants use sunlight energy, carbon dioxide gas from the air and water from the soil to make glucose, a type of sugar. This process is called photosynthesis, which means 'making from light'. You may have come across glucose in some sweets and drinks. Glucose gives plants the energy they need. It can be turned into different kinds of sugar and starches for storage and combined with minerals from the soil for plant growth.

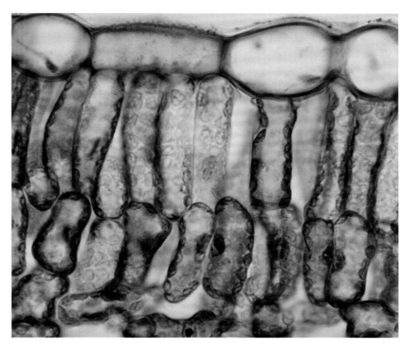

RIGHT *This magnified section through a plant leaf shows the tiny green chloroplasts inside the cells.*

It's good to be green

Photosynthesis takes place inside the cells of a leaf in tiny bodies called chloroplasts, which are too small to see without a microscope. They contain a chemical called chlorophyll, which only plants have. Chlorophyll gives plants their green colour and is used in photosynthesis to capture the energy of sunlight.

As well as making food for the plant photosynthesis also produces oxygen. Practically every living thing needs oxygen to stay alive, so this is another vital role plants play in the living world. Without plants and photosynthesis there would be no life as we know it.

LEFT *Plants are a source of food for the world's animals, such as this African lowland gorilla in the Democratic Republic of the Congo.*

WOW!

On average photosynthesis produces 240 billion tonnes of new plant material every year across the world. In a year, one square metre of rainforest will produce the energy equivalent of 2.5 kilograms of sugar.

Specialized leaves

Leaves aren't just food factories. They can be the plant's toolbox, carrying out many important tasks, including support and protection.

Twining tendrils

Some of the leaves of climbing plants are threadlike and coiling. These tendrils circle slowly in the air until they find something to cling on to and then they wind themselves around it. This gives the plant support as it climbs upwards. Peas, grape vines and ivy all produce tendrils.

Swollen leaves

Succulents are plants that live in dry places and their thick, swollen leaves are adapted to store water. The leaves are either hairy or waxy to help reduce water loss. Succulents include house leeks, stonecrops and odd-looking plants called living stones.

LEFT *The snow pea plant grows tendrils that twine around things, such as a fence or the branching stem of another plant.*

WOW!

The world's biggest cactus is the giant saguaro, which can grow up to 20 metres tall. It can store around six tonnes of water inside its stem.

Cactus spines

At first glance a cactus might not appear to have any leaves, but in fact it does. Its leaves have become clusters of spines dotted around its thick stem. Cacti are a type of succulent, storing water in their stems rather than their leaves.

The leaves serve a double purpose. Cacti grow in hot, dry places and having leaves that are very much reduced in size helps to cut down on water loss. The sharp spines also give the cactus some protection from desert animals that try to eat it.

Drip-tips and water wings

Plants that live in very damp conditions also have special leaf adaptations. The weight of too much rainwater might be enough to break the branches of a tree so rainforest trees have leaves with pointed tips that turn downwards. These 'drip-tips' make it easy for rainwater to run off the leaves.

The big floating leaves of water lilies are filled with air spaces. The air trapped inside acts like water wings, keeping the leaf afloat on the surface of the pond. A water-repellent waxy substance covers the top of the leaf. This helps to prevent the leaf from being sunk by water collecting on it.

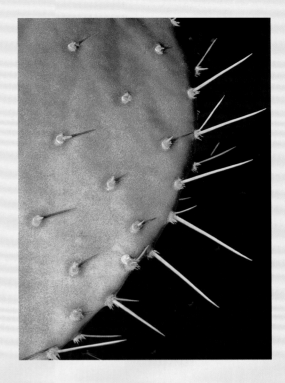

ABOVE *Needle-like leaves protect this cactus from hungry animals and also help to prevent water loss.*

Insect eaters

Some plants that live in poor soils add to their diet by capturing insects. The Venus flytrap has leaves that are hinged down the middle. If an insect lands on the leaf the two halves snap shut, trapping it inside. Curved spines around the outside of the leaf stop the doomed insect from escaping.

LEFT *The two halves of a leaf on this Venus flytrap are about to snap shut around an ant, which it will later digest as food.*

Plant defences

Plants can't pull up their roots and escape if something starts to eat them. But some of them have a few defences to rely on – some are obvious and others not so obvious.

ABOVE *The grasslands of Africa are nibbled by countless grazing animals, such as these wildebeest in Kenya, but the grasses still grow back.*

Keep growing

Unlike animals, plants can lose large parts and still keep growing. Grasses, for example, grow from the base of their leaves, down near the soil, and not from the tip. So no matter how much an animal nibbles away at the grass, as long as some green part remains the grass will grow back again.

Thorns, spines and prickles

We have already come across the spiny leaves of the cactus, and other plants are armed for survival, too. Whereas spines are specialized leaves, thorns are specialized short stems that end in a sharp point. The hawthorn is an example of a plant that is well-equipped with thorns. Although we often talk about roses having thorns they actually have prickles. The difference is that a prickle is attached to the surface of the stem and breaks off fairly easily.

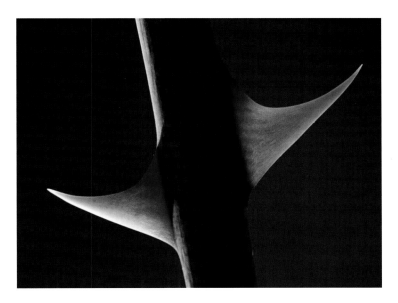

ABOVE *The stem of a dog rose has sharp prickles which stop animals eating it.*

ABOVE *Plants that are attacked by insects may release chemicals that attract predators like this soldier bug, which then kill the plant eaters.*

Chemical defences

Many plants have less obvious, but just as effective, ways of defending themselves. They use chemical weapons. The variety of these defences is quite astonishing. Some plants produce chemicals that repel insects and other animals, discouraging them from feeding or laying their eggs. Others produce poisons that kill a feeding insect.

Some plants produce chemicals that interfere with an insect's development so it doesn't grow up as it should. Other plant chemicals can stop an insect's digestive system from working properly so it starves. Some plants can mimic insect alarm scents so they flee as if there was an insect-eating predator present. There is non-stop chemical warfare in the plant world!

Flowers

What makes flowering plants different from other plants is their flowers. There are a huge variety of flower shapes, scents and colours. They can be single or in huge clusters. So what exactly is a flower?

A new generation

A flower is a flowering plant's reproductive organ. Its purpose is to make sure that the plant can produce seeds which eventually grow into new plants.

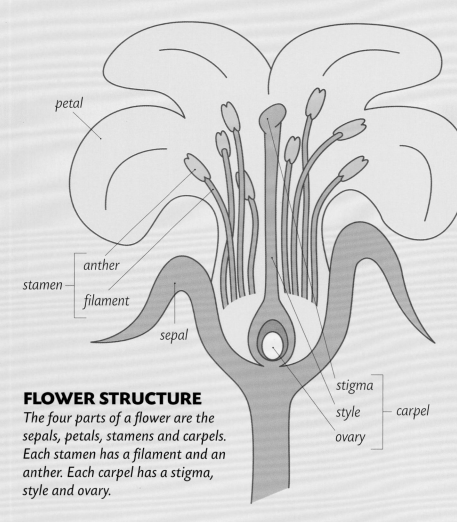

petal

anther

stamen

filament

sepal

stigma

style

ovary

carpel

FLOWER STRUCTURE

The four parts of a flower are the sepals, petals, stamens and carpels. Each stamen has a filament and an anther. Each carpel has a stigma, style and ovary.

Parts of a flower

Flowers develop from buds growing along the plant stem. A flower is really a collection of very specialized leaves. Most types of flower have four main parts: sepals, petals, stamens and carpels. The sepals are the green parts on the outside of the flower. They protect the flower bud and sometimes drop off after it opens. The petals are usually the most colourful parts of a flower. Inside the petals are the stamens and the carpels.

The stamens are the male parts of a flower; each stamen has a long narrow stalk called a filament, on the end of which is an anther. The anther produces the flower's pollen, which looks like fine dust. The carpels are the female parts of the flower. Each carpel has a stigma at the top, a stalk called a style and an ovary at the bottom that produces the ovules that will eventually form seeds.

The flowers of some types of plant contain both male and female parts. Other types grow separate male and female flowers on the same individual plant. There are also types in which there are male flowers on one plant and female flowers on another.

Florets and colourful leaves

Some flowers which look like single flowers, such as daisies, dandelions and sunflowers, are not single at all. They are made up of a tightly packed mass of very tiny flowers, called florets. What look like petals are colourful leaves called bracts that form a cup around the cluster of florets. Some flowering plants, such as poinsettias, have bracts that are more brightly coloured than the flowers.

ABOVE *Long male catkins and smaller red female flowers grow beside each other on this common alder tree.*

ABOVE *This sunflower is not a single flower at all, but is made up of a great many small florets packed closely together.*

WOW!

The biggest flower in the world is the stinking corpse lily, a parasite which grows in the tropical forests of South-east Asia. It is nearly a metre across and, as you might guess from the name, it doesn't smell very nice!

A new generation

Before a flower can produce seeds, pollen from male anthers has to reach its female stigma. This process is called pollination and it involves one of nature's most important partnerships.

Some plants can pollinate their own flowers. Pollen from a flower reaches the ovary on the same flower or an ovary in another flower on the same plant. This is called self-pollination. Other types of flower need pollen from another plant of the same kind. This is called cross-pollination and is done by a pollinator, such as the wind or an animal.

WOW!

The wind can carry pollen a very long way. Oak tree pollen has been found in the middle of the Atlantic Ocean, hundreds of kilometres from land.

This beach grass on a sand dune in Germany is pollinated by the wind.

On the wind
Flowers that need the wind to carry their pollen long distances have very long anthers and produce masses of lightweight pollen. Wind-pollinated flowers are often very small and may have tiny petals or no petals at all. Grasses and many types of tree are wind-pollinated.

Flowers and animals
Flower petals are often brightly coloured. They may also produce fragrant oils that give the flower a pleasing smell. This show of sights and smells attracts animal pollinators.

The main animal pollinators are insects, although birds and bats may also play a part. Flowers and insects work well together. The flower needs to be pollinated and the insect needs food. The flower produces a sweet, sugary, energy-giving liquid called nectar, which the insect drinks.

To reach the nectar an insect brushes against the flower's stamens and collects pollen grains on its hairy body. When the insect visits another flower the insect touches the stigma and leaves some pollen grains behind. When this happens the flower is pollinated.

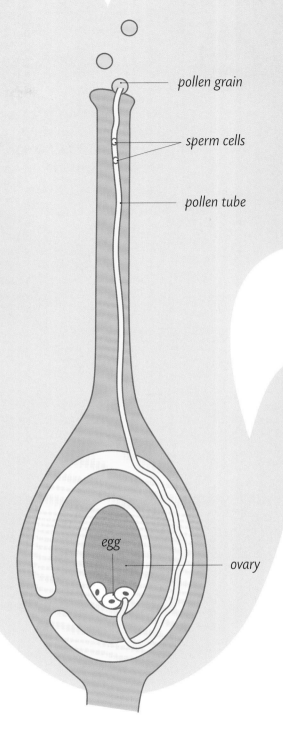

pollen grain

sperm cells

pollen tube

egg

ovary

LEFT *When an insect such as this bumblebee visits a flower it feeds on the nectar and collects pollen on its body.*

Setting seed

Now the flower can produce seeds. When the pollen grain reaches the stigma it begins to grow a very fine tube. This passes down through the style until it reaches the ovule inside the ovary. Tiny sperm cells move down the tube to fertilize the ovule. Now it can become a seed.

WOW!

A corn pollen tube might have to grow over 20 centimetres to reach the ovule and complete fertilization.

POLLEN TUBE

A pollen grain releases two sperm cells, which move downwards through a pollen tube to the ovary. One will fertilize an egg to form a new plant embryo; the other will form the embryo's food source.

Seeds and fruits

Seeds come in a large assortment of shapes and sizes. They may be so small and light they float in the air, or so big that they weigh several kilograms. Inside all of them are the beginnings of a new plant.

Seed parts

Inside the seed of every flowering plant there is an embryo, formed when the sperm cells from the pollen grain fertilized the ovule. The embryo is usually surrounded by a store of food made up of energy-rich starch and other substances. All this is enclosed within a protective seed coat.

Many flowering plant embryos also have either one or two seed leaves as food stores. These can take up most of the space inside the seed. Grasses, orchids and palm trees all have one seed leaf, while oak trees, beans and sunflowers have two seed leaves.

LEFT *The wings of this maple seed keep it in the air longer so it can land further from the parent tree.*

Fruit formation

After the seeds are produced the flower's carpels turn into fruits. Only flowering plants have fruits; no other type of plant does. When you think of fruit, apples, oranges and pears might come to mind. But the pod of a pea is also a fruit, and so are a cucumber and the little parachutes that blow off a dandelion head.

LEFT *The seeds of an orchid are so tiny and light they can be carried on the wind.*

Spreading seeds

Fruits have two jobs. One is to protect the seeds and the other is to make sure the seeds are spread as widely as possible. Spreading seeds is called dispersal.

The fruits of the sycamore tree spin like tiny propeller blades as they fall. This helps them to stay in the air longer so they travel further from the tree. Feathery dandelion parachutes are also carried by the wind. Some fruits burst as they dry out, spraying seeds in all directions.

Animals carry many seeds and fruits. Some fruits, such the burdock, have hooks that stick to an animal's fur as it brushes past the plant. Other plants have colourful fruits that are good to eat. The animal eats the fruit but does not digest the seeds inside and they pass out unharmed in its droppings. The droppings may even provide a natural fertilizer for the seed to grow!

ABOVE *These waxwings are feasting on berries and will leave the seeds in their droppings.*

WOW!

The world's biggest seeds belong to the coco de mer, a palm tree which grows on the Seychelles Islands in the Indian Ocean. These coconuts of the sea can be nearly a metre around and weigh 18 kilograms or more. The smallest seeds are those of orchids – a million would weigh less than a gram.

Time to grow

Most seeds go through a quiet phase of inactivity, or dormancy, when not much seems to be happening. When conditions are right the embryo inside will start to grow. This is germination.

Springing to life

Seeds do not usually start growing straight away. They need the right temperature and the right amount of moisture. In places where winters are cold the seeds may wait until the warmth of spring before germinating. Most seeds grow best at temperatures between 18 and 29°C. In dry areas seeds do not germinate until the rains come. Moisture is important because it softens the seed coat so the embryo growing inside can break out.

Primary roots

The first thing to emerge from the seed is the primary root, or radicle. The radicle is important because the one thing that isn't stored in the seed is water. It pushes down into the soil to begin drawing up water and minerals for the germinating seed. Once the root is established the shoot begins to grow.

STAGES OF GERMINATION
The first stages in the growth of a new plant change a seed into a seedling.

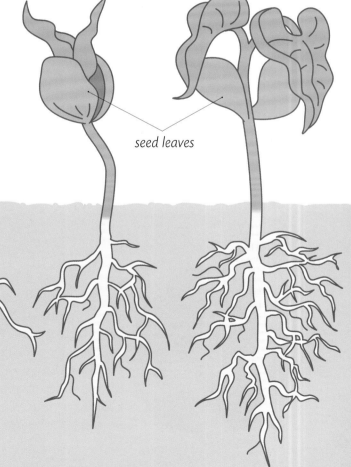

seed leaves

radicle

seed

From seed to seedling

The shoot that pushes up towards the light must not be damaged. Many plant shoots have stems which bend to form a loop so that the side of the stem comes up through the soil first. This helps to protect the delicate bud at the tip of the shoot.

The seed leaves of some plants stay beneath the ground, providing food for the growing shoot. Other kinds of plant have seed leaves which appear first above ground. They usually look different from the leaves the plant will grow later. As the new seedling's leaves begin to grow they provide it with food by photosynthesis. The seedling no longer needs the food stored in the seed leaves and they wither away. The seed has become a new young plant.

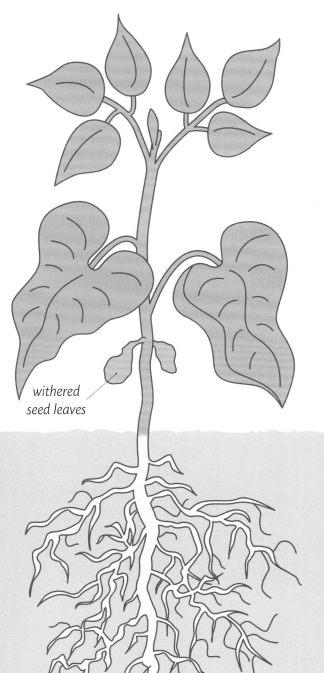

withered
seed leaves

WOW!

Some seeds can stay dormant longer than others before they germinate. The seeds of some maples die unless they germinate within two weeks. At the other extreme, 2,000-year-old seeds from lotus plants have successfully germinated.

Floral planet

It is hard to imagine what the world would be without flowers. It would certainly be a much less colourful place. It would be a very much quieter place, too, as the animals would starve with nothing to eat.

A multitude of flowers

Flowering plants live all over the world. There are flowers in the forests, flowers in the deserts and flowers on the sides of mountains. We bring flowers into our parks, gardens and homes. The only places without flowers are the iciest wildernesses of the polar regions.

The flowers these plants produce range from metre-wide, foul-smelling monstrosities to tiny blooms less than a millimetre across. Whatever their size and colour all flowers are there for the same reason, and that is to produce the seeds that will grow into the next generation of flowering plants.

The Mojave Desert in California bursts into flower after the short winter rains. A Joshua tree stands above a carpet of flowering Californian poppies.

BELOW *When the logging companies cut down trees and clear the forests they threaten not only plants, but also the animals that depend on the plants for food and shelter.*

Primary producers

There are more flowering plants than all the other types of plant put together. Their role in the living world is vital. Because flowering plants make their own food through photosynthesis they are sometimes called primary producers. Plants are the basis of nearly every food chain. They capture the energy that other living things depend on. If an animal doesn't eat plants itself it will certainly eat another animal that did eat plants. In the process of making food plants also produce oxygen, without which we could not survive.

Plants and us

We rely on flowering plants for many things. Four-fifths of the food eaten by the world's human population – all the cereal and all the fruit and vegetables – comes from flowering plants. We use wood from trees for fuel and for building and we use fibres from plants such as cotton to make clothes. Flowering plants are also a source of many medicines.

Pollution and the loss of habitats threaten the well-being of plants just as much as they affect other living things. If a plant becomes extinct so do the animals that feed on that plant, and the animals that feed on them. If you cut the first link in the chain the whole world begins to fall apart.

Glossary

Adaptation A feature of a living thing that makes it better suited to its lifestyle.

Anther The part of a flower where male pollen is produced.

Bud An undeveloped shoot or flower that has not yet opened out.

Carpel The female part of a flower that is made up of the stigma, style and ovary.

Chlorophyll A chemical that captures sunlight energy for use in photosynthesis and gives plants their green colour.

Conifer A type of evergreen tree that produces seeds in cones rather than flowers.

Cuticle A waxy protective layer on the outside of a leaf.

Embryo The young plant inside a seed.

Fertilize To make an ovule fertile; sperm cells in pollen grain fertilize an ovule so that a seed can grow.

Florets Tiny flowers that make up the flowerheads of plants such as sunflowers.

Foliage The leaves of a plant.

Food chain The relationship between living things that shows who gets eaten by whom.

Fronds The leaves of ferns.

Germination The growth of a seed when it starts to become a new plant.

Glucose A type of sugar produced by plants during photosynthesis.

Gymnosperm A type of plant, such as a conifer, that produces seeds that are not protected inside fruits.

Minerals Simple chemical substances that living things need to stay healthy. Plants get their minerals from the soil.

Nectar A sweet, energy-rich substance produced by many flowering plants to attract insects and other animals.

Ovary Part of the carpel where the ovules are and where seeds form.

Ovule Part of the ovary inside a carpel that develops into a seed after fertilization.

Parasite An organism that lives in or on another living thing, taking nourishment and causing harm.

Petiole The stalk that joins a leaf to the stem of a plant.

Phloem Tubes that carry minerals and sugar from one part of the plant to another.

Photosynthesis The process by which plants make sugar from sunlight energy, carbon dioxide and water.

Pollen Tiny grains produced in the male anthers of flowers; pollen must be carried to a stigma for pollination to take place.

Pollination The transfer of pollen from the male anther to the female stigma. Most flowers are pollinated by insects or the wind.

Pores Tiny openings in the surfaces of leaves that let air in and moisture out.

Radicle The first root to grow from a seed when it germinates.

Runner A slender stem that grows from the base of a plant to produce new plants.

Sepals Parts of a flower that protect the bud before it opens.

Spores The seeds of plants such as ferns and mosses; a spore grows into a new plant if conditions are right.

Stamen The male part of a flower that is made up of an anther on a long filament.

Starch A substance plants produce from the sugar they make during photosynthesis; starch can be stored in roots, seeds and fruit as a source of energy.

Stem The part of a plant that connects its roots to its leaves and flowers; it carries water and food between the different parts.

Stigma The sticky top of the female carpel that captures the pollen grains.

Xylem Tubes that carry water to the different parts of a plant.

Websites

http://waynesword.palomar.edu/trmar98.htm
A colourful introduction to the world of flowering plants.

http://www.kidsgardening.com/growingideas/projects/jan03/pg1.html
Ideas for creating a pollinator garden to bring flowers and insects together.

http://photoscience.la.asu.edu/photosyn/education/learn.html#amazing
What is photosynthesis? An Arizona State University site with links to many articles on photosynthesis.

http://www.plantlife.org.uk/
Plantlife International works for the conservation of wild plants throughout the world.

Index

PILLGWENLLY

23-07-18